A SAVIOUR
IS PROMISED

A STUDY IN ISAIAH 1–39

BIBLE STUDIES TO IMPACT THE LIVES
OF ORDINARY PEOPLE

Christian Focus Publications

The Word Worldwide

Written by John Priddle

PREFACE

GEARED FOR GROWTH

'Where there's LIFE there's GROWTH:
Where there's GROWTH there's LIFE.'

WHY GROW a study group?

Because as we study the Bible and share together we can

- learn to combat loneliness, depression, staleness, frustration, and other problems
- get to understand and love each other
- become responsive to the Holy Spirit's dealing and obedient to God's Word

and that's GROWTH.

How do you GROW a study group?

- Just start by asking a friend to join you and then aim at expanding your group.
- Study the set portions daily (they are brief and easy: no catches).
- Meet once a week to discuss what you find.
- Befriend others, both Christians and non Christians, and work away together

see how it GROWS!

WHEN you GROW ...

This will happen at school, at home, at work, at play, in your youth group, your student fellowship, women's meetings, mid-week meetings, churches and communities,

you'll be REACHING THROUGH TEACHING

INTRODUCTORY STUDY

Is Isaiah a book or a person?

Well, both are true. The book Isaiah contains the message which God gave the man, Isaiah, to pass on to His people. We can obtain a profile of Isaiah by looking up the following references:

Where did he live? _?_   *Isaiah 7:1-3*
Was he married? _Yes_   8:3
Who was his elder son? _Shear-Jashub_   7:3
And his younger son? _Maher-Shalal-Hash-Baz_   8:3
What was his vocation? _Prophet (telling the people what God says)_   6:8
How many kings reigned in his lifetime? _4_   1:1
What was his warning to his people? _what happen as turned against_ 3:8 _God_
Why was God going to bring judgment? _Left God, turned away; as if He was ashamed_   1:4; 3:9 _Proud of their sin don't care who sees it_
What wonderful future event did he prophesy?   7:14; 9:6
Birth of Christ Jesus   _Full of Sin / Doing Evil_

Isaiah, along with Amos, Hosea and Micah, is important, because he stands on the threshold of a new era, not only of Israel's story, but of world history.

Up to this point in time the world had been comprised of small, independent tribes and nations occasionally conquering or being conquered, yet never on a massive scale. But looming on the horizon there is first one great power, Assyria, and then lurking in the shadows, an even greater power, Babylon. About this time also the legendary foundation of the city of Rome was laid.

Thought Imagine Isaiah (or a present-day man of God) declaring to this nation 'Oh, sinful nation, a people loaded with guilt, a brood of evildoers, children given to corruption. You have forsaken the Lord; you have spurned the Holy One and turned your backs on Him.'

Discuss:

1) How valid is this statement for our nation today? _-Totally_
2) Imagine what the general reaction would be. _- Religious Cult; Dangerous; Problems will obey; Cause No truth_
3) Describe your own personal feelings and reaction to such a message. _Neglience_
All true - but people aren't loaded with guilt
Depressed - pulls / counsellors; self-thinking; thinking of the moment now

Read Isaiah 6:1-8 aloud twice and then discuss:

How did God 'call' Isaiah to be a prophet? _Vision_
What impressed Isaiah most about God?
What did this make him realise about himself? _- He was not pure - not able to_
Why is it important for us to be aware of these facts about God and ourselves _come into God's presence_
too?

? Chpt 7.15   _? 9 v. 7._

Isaiah's vision coloured all his future teaching. Consider these verses: Isaiah 5:24; 10:17, 20; 12:6; 17:7; 29:19; 30:11, 12a, 15; 31:1

God's standard is HOLINESS. In Exodus 3:5, 6 we see God glorious in His holiness; throughout the New Testament Jesus is recognised as the Holy One of God (Rev. 3:7); and the teaching on the standards for His church is holiness (Eph. 5:26, 27). As we study this book may the Lord give us a fresh vision of His holiness and so work in us by His Spirit that our consuming passion will be for holiness – 'without holiness no-one will see the Lord' (Heb. 12:14).

Isaiah shows not only the judgment of God, but His plan of salvation and grace. During the next 12 weeks we will study the first 39 chapters of Isaiah.

It is interesting to note:

The Bible consists of 66 books,
   39 Old Testament and 27 New Testament.

Isaiah has 66 chapters,
   39 dealing with Israel before exile
      and 27 dealing with deliverance from exile.

Encourage one another to underline and memorise as many as possible of the wonderful texts in this rich storehouse of spiritual treasure. Familiarise yourself with the world of Isaiah's day, locating on a map the countries and peoples mentioned in these studies week by week.

ISAIAH'S WORLD

MEDIA

ELAM

Persian Gulf

●BABYLON

Nineveh●

R. Tigris

R. Euphrates

●Tadmor

Desert

ARPAD

●Hamath

●Damascus

MOAB

Aradus●

Byblus●

SIDON

Tyre●

Mt. Carmel

Samaria●

Cyprus

Jerusalem●

Ashdod●

EDOM

●Elath

Red Sea

SINAI

Mediterranean Sea

ZOAN Pelusium

Gulf of Suez

Memphis●

Nile R.

Hanes●

STUDY 1

HARD TIMES AHEAD

QUESTIONS

DAY 1 *Isaiah 1:1-9.*
a) What humiliating contrast do you see in verses 2-3?
b) Compare and contrast the fate of Judah with that of Sodom and Gomorrah (Gen. 19:24-29).

DAY 2 *Isaiah 1:10-15.*
a) Who are being addressed in verse 10?
b) Describe the two attitudes of God presented in verse 14 and give the reasons for them. *~ Weariness at their continued Sinning*

hate?

DAY 3 *Isaiah 1:16-20.*
a) What particular evils must be put right (vv. 16, 17)? *injustice lack of concern for the helpless*
b) What great promise is here? What does it mean for us today (1 John 1:9)? *Seek Justice Help Orphans Stand up for rights of widows*

DAY 4 *Isaiah 1:21-31.*
a) What pictures describe Israel's sorry condition?
b) What two particular evils are portrayed in verses 23-29? *orphan widow*
c) God's judgment must fall, but what is His ultimate purpose? *to seek repentance in the wrong doer; cleanse/free them - Salvation*

DAY 5 *Compare Isaiah 2:1-4 with Micah 4:1-5.*
a) Do you think Isaiah saw this happen in his day? What connection might Acts 1:8 have with this passage in Isaiah?
b) How is it possible to see Revelation 21:2, 10, 11, 22-25 as one fulfilment of Isaiah's vision?

DAY 6 *Isaiah 2:5-11.*
a) What challenge immediately follows the vision of verses 1-4? Discuss the relation of Psalm 119:105 to this challenge.
b) What evils were denounced? What would happen to the unrepentant?

DAY 7 *Isaiah 2:12-22.*
A common idea in Israel was that the Day of the Lord would be a time when God would intervene and slaughter their enemies. In fact, who are being judged here?

Try to memorise: Isaiah 1:18.

[margin handwritten notes:] Look up 'Hate' in Concordance — v 14. 'Disust'?

If you turn to God's way, obey His will. We will be as much washed white as — cleansed/forgiven.

NOTES

Afflicted – in vain?
One can discern the yearning heart of our Father God as He grieves over Israel, His children.

You are the children of the Lᴏʀᴅ your God ...
you are a people holy to the Lᴏʀᴅ your God.
Out of all the peoples on the face of the earth,
the Lᴏʀᴅ has chosen you to be His treasured possession (Deut. 14:1-2).

Read Moses' song about Israel in Deuteronomy 32 to recall all the wonderful things God had done for them. Isaiah's cry about God's people is very different! Isaiah 1:21-23 is a lament over Israel's sin. Ungodliness is everywhere. God's response is very definite: 'I will turn my hand against you; I will thoroughly purge away your dross and remove all your impurities' (v. 25).

Life isn't meant to be easy
Scripture does not indicate that the Christian pathway will be a continual bed of roses. Rather, the message is clear that the way to spiritual growth is through trial and testing.
    In James 1:1-4 there is a message to the 'twelve tribes scattered among the nations' and this does not only mean historical Israel, but all who have become God's children through faith in Christ's redeeming sacrifice: 'Consider it pure joy, my brothers, whenever you face trials of many kinds, because you know that the testing of your faith develops perseverance. Perseverance must finish its work so that you may be mature and complete, not lacking anything.'

The cost of sonship
God calls Israel, 'my children, my sons'. Listen to these words from Hebrews 12:5-7: 'And you have forgotten that word of encouragement that addresses you as sons: "My son, do not make light of the Lord's discipline, and do not lose heart when he rebukes you, because the Lord disciplines those he loves, and he punishes everyone he accepts as a son." Endure hardship as a discipline; God is treating you as sons.'
    As we study on through Isaiah and trace God's loving but disciplining hand on the nations of the Old Testament world, we will learn to more fully understand His working in the world today and to accept His overruling purposes in our own lives.

God's mouthpiece
Isaiah had a difficult task. Communing with God, knowing His heart's desire for

Israel, yet seeing over and over again their rebellion and idolatry, his heart too must have been broken. He was human too. He must have been sometimes tempted to 'throw in the sponge' as it were. What held him to his commission? The vision he received from God (Isa. 6) was vivid and vital. The assurance that God had called him and would continue to guide and keep him was his mainstay, and the mainstay of other prophets who followed.

The situations in which he lived and worked had an 'up and down' quality about them. Elated, as God gave repeated promises that He would yet bless His wayward people, sad when he saw Israel stubbornly persist in sin, he pressed on steadily in the task. God gave him that glorious vision of a future day when Israel would dwell, forgiven and at peace with God in Jerusalem (Isa. 2:2-4) and His Word would be proclaimed from there. Isaiah did not live to see that day, but we read of it in Acts 1:8 and Peter declares it in Acts 2:2-21. The same prophecy is given also in Joel 2:28.

STUDY 2
SOWING AND REAPING

QUESTIONS

DAY 1 *Isaiah 3:1-15.*
a) Discuss the signs of anarchy and lawlessness here (vv. 4-9, 12, 14).
b) In this chaotic situation, whom will God protect (v. 10)?
c) Who, in particular, are condemned (vv. 14, 15)?

DAY 2 *Isaiah 3:16-4:1.*
a) Find the chief reason for the condemning of the women (vv. 15, 16).
b) What is the greatest indignity threatened (4:1)?

DAY 3 *Isaiah 4:2-6.*
a) Who will remove the sin of the people of Jerusalem?
b) What else would be done for Jerusalem?

DAY 4 *Isaiah 5:1-7.*
a) What went wrong in this vineyard?
b) What kind of fruit does God always want in our lives (John 15:1-9)?
c) What does the poor fruit in Isaiah's story represent (v. 7)?

DAY 5 *Isaiah 5:8-17.*
a) What two evils are mentioned here?
b) What will these evils bring on the people?

DAY 6 *Isaiah 5:18-25.*
a) List at least four more evils mentioned here.
b) What sin is at the root of them all (v. 24)?
c) Discuss the existence today of the sins mentioned in verses 8-25.

DAY 7 *Isaiah 5:26-30.*
a) What method was God going to use to bring judgment on those who opposed Him?
b) Can you identify the nation which would be involved in this (Isa. 8:7-8; 10:5-6)?

A good passage to memorise: Isaiah 4:5-6.

NOTES

Those who sow trouble reap it (Job 4:8)
Look up Psalm 126:5; Hosea 8:7; 10:12; Romans 6:22; 2 Corinthians 9:6: Galatians 6:7. You can probably find other references to bear out the point that we all reap what we sow. The Jews had left God out of their thinking. Now they feel that everything they had pinned their hopes on had vanished. Above all, they had lost their respected leaders. Now there was to be chaos. One of the signs of decadence is the self-indulgence and show of the women. They are in for quite a surprise! Worst of all, seven of them will be fighting over one man for the privilege of being his wife.

A flash of hope
Isaiah breaks into this gloomy picture with the wonderful prediction that there is a bright future ahead for God's children (Isa. 4:2-6). The time may be years away, but to those who accept this word from God the prospect is good and encouraging.

You are doomed
When the Lord Jesus recounted the parable in Mark 12:1-12 there was strong reaction from the teachers of the law. The message condemned them. Isaiah used the same method here and gained a sympathetic audience. Then they realised he was not speaking of a literal vineyard. When he applied the meaning, the message must have shot right home. In chapter 5 in the Good News Bible the message of doom is constantly repeated (vv. 8, 11, 18, 20, 21, 22).

Fruit
God was looking for the good fruits of love, justice and obedience in His people. Instead, He found the bitter fruit of oppression, drunkenness, blasphemy, etc. The result is inevitable: the people will only reap what they have sown. God will bring His purposes about by allowing the Assyrians to swoop in and devastate the land. Would this make Israel listen?

How are we doing?
Are we listening, responding and producing good fruit? Or is the Lord disappointed in the quality of our lives? Galatians 5:19-25 speaks very clearly of the choice set before us. Our lives will be pleasing to God and manifesting the fruit of the Spirit as we yield to His will and do not walk in disobedience.

> Sow flowers, and flowers will blossom
> Around you, wherever you go.
> Sow weeds and of weeds reap the harvest
> You reap whatever you sow.

STUDY 3
WHO WILL GO?

QUESTIONS

DAY 1 *Isaiah 6:1-7; 2 Chronicles 26:19-21.*
a) What brought about Isaiah's confession of sin?
b) How did God respond?
c) What is promised to us in 1 John 1:9?

DAY 2 *Isaiah 6:8-13.*
a) What happened next to Isaiah?
b) Was Isaiah promised a successful ministry? What caused Paul to quote from Isaiah in Acts 26:23-27?

DAY 3 *Isaiah 7:1-9.*
a) How does the Lord describe Judah's enemies (vv. 1, 4)?
b) Read verses 4, 5, 9 in several translations. What do we learn about Pekah?
c) What was to be the 'secret' of Ahaz's success (and ours too when faced with opposition)?

DAY 4 *Isaiah 7:10-16; Matthew 1:21-23.*
a) Discuss the wonderful prophecy found here.
b) What does 'Immanuel' mean?

DAY 5 *Isaiah 7:17-25, 2 Kings 16:5-9.*
a) How is the coming invasion described?
b) Who controls all these invaders? What is the message for Israel?
c) Why does it seem ironical that Assyria is to be the invader?

DAY 6 *Isaiah 8:1-8.*
a) When was this child born?
b) How is the Assyrian attack described?
c) What gleam of hope is there in verse 8?

DAY 7 *Isaiah 8:9-22; 2 Peter 1:19-21.*
a) Find the statement used to defy Israel's enemies (v. 10).
b) When people ignore God what are they tempted to do?
c) What has God given to guide His people?

Yet another memory verse: Isaiah 6:8.

NOTES

Uzziah became King when he was 16 and reigned for 52 years. The country prospered under his rule and he was almost as rich and prosperous as King Solomon. We read in 2 Chronicles 26:5 that as long as he sought the Lord, God made him to prosper. However, with riches and power he allowed pride to fill his heart. In arrogance he went to the temple to burn incense, a duty usually only performed by the priest. Despite the advice of the chief priest, Azariah and 80 others, he persisted. Because of his self-will, God struck him with leprosy and he suffered with this disease until he died (2 Chron. 26:16-21).

Perhaps it was this tragedy which brought Isaiah to the temple. There he had the vision recounted in chapter 6. It is possible he was burdened and praying about what would happen in the nation now that Uzziah was dead.

I saw the Lord ...

Isaiah was obviously very much in the presence of the Lord. No doubt there was clamour all around him, but he was 'shut in' with his Creator. Uzziah had entered the temple presumptuously. Even the seraphs had to hide their faces from the glory of the Lord.

But Isaiah was groaning in despair: 'Woe to me ... I am a man of unclean lips ... my eyes have seen the King, the LORD Almighty'. His acknowledgement of sin and unworthiness brought God's mercy to bear. He was not consumed or stricken with disease. He was assured of forgiveness and challenged with a need. What an ordination for his life work: 'Go and tell this people'.

God warned Isaiah that the people would not listen to him, but the vision in the temple gave him confidence to faithfully, persistently, proclaim God's word.

Contrasts: obedience v disobedience

Jotham, Uzziah's son, acted as regent during his father's long illness and then became king when his father died. That was approximately the time when Isaiah began his great ministry (6:1). No doubt he greatly influenced Jotham (2 Kings 15:32-38; 2 Chron. 27), whom God blessed because of his faithful walk with Him (2 Chron. 27:6).

Ahaz, Jotham's son, was only 20 when he became king, though he had been co-regent with his father for four years. When the kings of Damascus and Israel liaised to attack Judah, God sent Isaiah with a message for Ahaz (Isa. 7:1-9), but he refused to go God's way, and things went from bad to worse in Judah.

Ahaz looked for help in the wrong direction (2 Chron. 28:20) and this pushed him into increasing apostasy (2 Kings 16:3, 4; 2 Chron. 28:23). When he died he was not buried in regal honour (2 Chron. 28:27).

Blind Spots!
If only Ahaz had soaked up God's word through Isaiah. What a wonderful promise he glossed over (Isa. 7:14), covering over his unbelief with a hypocritical attitude. What calamity he brought on the nation, leading them into apostasy.

We need to take heed to respond correctly to the truth of God's Word. Yet human nature is such that we are prone to look almost anywhere except to God when we get into a tight spot.

STUDY 4
THE PRINCE OF PEACE

QUESTIONS

DAY 1 *Isaiah 9:1-7; Matthew 4:12-16.*
a) What evils will the Promised One remove?
b) Discuss the characteristics of God as revealed in verse 6.

DAY 2 *Isaiah 9:8-21.*
a) List some of the reactions to God's warnings.
b) State the recurring refrain in this passage.

DAY 3 *Isaiah 10:1-11.*
a) What role had God intended for Assyria (v. 5)?
b) How did Assyria regard herself (v. 13)?
c) Discuss what Hebrews 12:7-11 teaches about God's disciplining of Christians.
Describe any experiences you may have had of this.

DAY 4 *Isaiah 10:12-19.*
a) How does God react to Assyria's boast (v. 15)?
b) When God deals with Assyria what will be left (v. 19) (2 Kings 19:35-37)?

DAY 5 *Isaiah 10:20-34.*
a) What earlier story are they reminded of in verses 26,27 (Exod. 14:16)?
b) After the military advance (vv. 28-32) who will stop Assyria (v. 33)? Describe the picture given.

DAY 6 *Isaiah 11:1-9.*
a) List the characteristics of the Messiah given here.
b) What extra truths are noted in addition to those mentioned in Isaiah 9:6-7?
c) Romans 8:22 speaks of creation groaning with pain. What signs are here given of a restored creation (vv. 6-9)?

DAY 7 *Isaiah 11:10-16.*
a) How will God unite the people (v. 10)?
b) What is the return of the people compared to in verse 16?

Memory verse: Isaiah 9:6.

NOTES

Immanuel – God with us
This is our only hope of eternal peace. This name must have brought glorious hope into the heart of Isaiah and the picture becomes increasingly clearer – He is to be the coming King, Wonderful Counsellor, Mighty God, Prince of Peace, ruling eternally. If only Israel could have seen, with the eyes of faith, the reality of this marvellous prophecy.

The word of God was given through Isaiah – a promise to look forward to with expectancy – 'The virgin ... will give birth to a son ...' (Isa. 7:14).

Just as they found it difficult to picture a coming event, so today's generation lacks the ability to grasp that this part of God's prophecy has been fulfilled. Christmas has been celebrated every year for nearly 2000 years, but the tinsel and toys obscure for many the eternal promise which can give life and peace.

Isaiah kept the vision in his heart while he coped with current issues. He saw Assyria as God's tool to punish Israel, but he also saw that God's judgment would fall on them for their cruelty and ferocity. They condemned themselves because of their pride in their own prowess and refusal to acknowledge a Sovereign God.

A future in God's plan
Assyria would pass away, but Israel would remain. Just as God had delivered them from Egypt, so He would deliver future generations.

Isaiah's refuge
Surely the Rock of Ages was Isaiah's hiding place in the fierceness of this struggle and despite Israel's trials, he knew that one day the Prince of Peace would bring peace to the nation. He had absolute confidence in the unchanging God – and we can have that too.

His name is Wonderful,
His name is Wonderful,
His name is Wonderful,
Jesus my Lord;
He is the mighty King,
Master of everything,
His name is Wonderful,
Jesus, my Lord.

He's the great Shepherd,
The Rock of all Ages,
Almighty God is He;
Bow down before Him,
Love and adore Him,
His name is Wonderful
Jesus my Lord.

(Copyright Manna Music Inc. U.S.A.)

STUDY 5
WHAT ABOUT OTHER NATIONS?

QUESTIONS

DAY 1 *Isaiah 12.*
a) How would the people react to God's intervention on their behalf?
b) Should we as individuals be experiencing any of these reactions?

DAY 2 *Isaiah 13:1-8.*
a) The picture of the banner calling people together or to battle has been seen in 5:26 (Assyria) and 11:12 (Judah and Israel). What is the purpose of the summons in verses 2-5 here?
b) Discuss what Ephesians 6:12 teaches us about the powers of evil.

DAY 3 *Isaiah 13:9-16.*
The judgment on Babylon is compared with a far greater judgment. What is this great event (Jude 14, 15; Rev. 20:12)?

DAY 4 *Isaiah 13:17-22.*
a) What particular sinful attitude is attributed to Babylon (v. 19)?
b) What was to be Babylon's fate (vv. 19-22)? (Rev. 18 is of interest here.)

DAY 5 *Isaiah 14:1-10.*
a) What promise does God have here for Israel (v. 1)?
b) Who would really break the power of Babylon (vv. 3-5)?

DAY 6 *Isaiah 14:11-23.*
a) What good reasons are there for this triumphant song (vv. 12, 15)?
b) Read Genesis 3:1-5; Matthew 4:8-9. How strongly do these verses support the view that Babylon is a picture of the world in opposition to God, and the King of Babylon a picture of Satan?

QUESTIONS (contd.)

DAY 7 *Isaiah 14:24-32.*
a) Describe God's plans and purposes for Assyria and others (v. 25).
b) How should this picture reassure us (vv. 26, 27)?

NOTES

Praiseful response
How readily and spontaneously do we rejoice and praise God for all He has done for us? Isaiah had his song of redemption and worship and it is recorded for God's children:

> Shout aloud and sing for joy, people of Zion,
> for great is the Holy One of Israel among you (Isa. 12:6).

The Penalty for Defiance
Isaiah prophesied Babylon's downfall about 700 BC. The city was repeatedly invaded and conquered over the next 300 years and by New Testament times this most splendid city in the world was reduced to a mound. Daniel 5:30 records how God used the Medes and the Persians as His instruments in her downfall. To this day she is desolate. 'Babylon Halt' is written in Arabic and English on the sign board of Baghdad railway station which lies four hundred yards from the ruins. The desolate yellowish brown ruins, marked by silent stillness or utter solitude remain a witness to Babylon's destruction.

The Tale of Two Cities
This describes Revelation 18 which tells of Jerusalem and Babylon, God's city and the Devil's. As you read the chapter (and it is not complete without chapter 21 – the positive side of the story) you will marvel that Isaiah's prediction about a city which was totally anti-God is now seen in the setting of God's final dealings with Satan and all the forces of evil. To date nearly 3,000 years have gone since Isaiah's time. Revelation 22:20 tells us Jesus is coming soon – to reign. Can you say 'Amen. Come, Lord Jesus'?

Sin is Sin
Babylon's sin was her pride and cruelty and Philistia and Assyria, guilty of the same atrocities, were to be judged in the same way. *Do we learn from history?* Despite these vivid accounts of our holy, just and loving God pleading for repentance and calling for a people who will walk in holiness, the same sins are rife in today's world – pride, cruelty and idolatry all play their part still.

Beware!
Even those of us who profess to be His children often want our own way. It is easy to plan our own course and fall into the trap of being 'on top' of things because all is going well. Sometimes pride can hinder us from turning to the Lord when we are conscious of needs in our lives. We, too, can be heedless of the needs of others.

Think of some of the subtle 'idols' we allow to take first place in our lives. Our questions, 'What about other nations? Or this nation?', need to narrow down to 'What about us? Me?' if we are to live with God first in our lives.

A well-known hymn expresses this graphically:

The dearest idol I have known
What e'er that idol be
Help me to tear it from Thy throne
And worship only Thee.

William Cowper

STUDY 6
SAVED OR LOST?

QUESTIONS

DAY 1 *Isaiah 15:1-9.*
a) Chapters 13-14 record Isaiah's song of judgment. What is different in chapter 15 (v. 5)?
b) How possible is it to feel sorrow for those who come under God's judgment (Matt. 23:37; Rom. 9:1-3)?

DAY 2 *Isaiah 16:1-6.*
a) If Moab appeals genuinely for help, what will happen (vv. 4b, 5)?
b) What is the basic reason for rejecting an appeal from Moab (v. 6)?

DAY 3 *Isaiah 16:7-14.*
a) Moab's pride and abundance are shown to be futile. What else is futile (v. 12)?
b) Can you suggest other nations that have totally disappeared as Moab did?

DAY 4 *Isaiah 17:1-6.* (Note that Damascus was the capital of Aram or Syria.)
a) Aram (Syria) lay between Assyria and Israel. What was to happen to this nation (v. 1)?
b) What three pictures are used to describe the fate of Northern Israel (vv. 4-6)? (Note: 'Ephraim' = Northern Israel.)

DAY 5 *Isaiah 17:7-11.*
a) What are the aims of God's judgments here (vv. 7, 8)?
b) What events seem to be recalled in verse 9 (Josh. 11:23)?
c) What is the cause of their problems now (v. 10)?

DAY 6 *Isaiah 17:12-14.*
a) What are the nations like as they attack (v. 12)?
b) What are they like when God has dealt with them (v. 13, 37:36)?

QUESTIONS (contd.)

DAY 7 *Isaiah 18:1-7.*
These verses refer to ambassadors (v. 2) from Sudan or Ethiopia hoping to form an alliance with Hezekiah against Assyria. What does the prophet refer to in verse 7? What happened in Acts 8:27-38?

NOTES

Moab
These people were descendants of Lot's grandson, Moab. Read about their beginnings in Genesis 19:30-38. They settled in the land east of Jordan (Num. 21:13-15) and refused Israel passage to Canaan (Judg. 11:17, 18). Their history reveals an anti-Israel attitude and yet they were really part of the nation. Moab was a great nephew of Abraham. Isaiah is well aware of this and grieves over Moab's fate. Yet God's judgment must fall on such an unrepentant nation. There is a similar picture of Abraham's pleading with God to spare Sodom from destruction (and so deliver his nephew Lot). Read the account in Genesis 18:19-33.

Syria
Also termed 'Aram', it lay north of Galilee, west of the Arabian desert and east of the Mediterranean Sea. David subdued Syria (2 Sam. 8:10) but she remained hostile to Israel (1 Kings 11:25). God used this nation to punish Joash (2 Chron. 24:23). Syria played a prominent part in the early Church. At Antioch the followers of Jesus were first called Christians (Acts 11:26). Paul was converted in Syria on the road to Damascus (Acts 9:1-9). It was here also that Paul and Barnabas were commissioned to take the gospel to the Gentiles (Acts 13:1-3).
   In Isaiah's day, however, Syria formed an alliance with Northern Israel or Ephraim against King Ahaz of Judah and Isaiah foretold their doom (see Isa. 7:5-9; 2 Kings 16:9; 17:5, 6 for a simple record of the facts). Syria's sin, like that of Moab, was idolatry.

Ephraim
Syria had been a buffer between Northern Israel and Assyria. After Syria was conquered it was not long before Israel followed. We read that 'the LORD was very angry with Israel and removed them from his presence' (2 Kings 17:18). You may wish to read the fuller account of this in 2 Kings 17:17-23. The following verses (24-34) explain how Samaria arose from the Northern Kingdom due to Assyrian resettlement.

Cush
Also known as Ethiopia or Sudan, was concerned about the Assyrian invasion. No mention is made of any gross sin but they are advised not to worry about human alliances against the enemy. God will deal with Assyria and they can return peacefully to their own land. This will eventually lead to the people returning to Jerusalem to worship and give thanks to God. Psalm 68:31 states this very thing and the account of the Ethiopian eunuch in Acts 8:27 bears it out.

God knows human nature. He deals with nations (and individuals John 1:12; Prov. 3:11, 12) in His own special way. Are you trusting Him to deal with your own nation? Knowing His unfailing purposes and unchangeable character should help us to pray aright for our leaders and country.

STUDY 7
GOD IS IN CONTROL

QUESTIONS

DAY 1 *Isaiah 19:1-15.*
a) In what way will the Lord judge Egypt?
b) Who in particular have failed to help Egypt (vv. 11, 12)?

DAY 2 *Isaiah 19:16-25.*
a) Why should Egypt fear Judah (vv. 16, 17)?
b) What great promises are yet to be fulfilled in Egypt (v. 25)?

DAY 3 *Isaiah 20:1-6.*
a) How did Isaiah demonstrate the folly of relying on other countries for help (vv. 3, 4)?
b) What conclusion would the people come to (v. 6)?
c) On whom should they have been relying (17:10)?

DAY 4 *Isaiah 21:1-10.*
a) How does the prophet react to the revelation of future judgment (vv. 3, 4)?
b) What message does the watchman receive (v. 9)? (Verse 8 is best read in various translations.)

DAY 5 *Isaiah 21:11-17.*
a) What advice given to Dumah (Edom) is applicable to us today?
b) How long will it be till morning? (See 2 Thess. 1:6-10 for possible New Testament parallels.)

DAY 6 *Isaiah 22:1-14.*
a) What was basically wrong with the nation (vv. 9-13)?
b) How would God react to these attitudes (v. 14)?

DAY 7 *Isaiah 22:15-25.*
a) Why was Shebna being condemned (v. 16)?
b) What does Isaiah 36:3; 37:2 suggest about Shebna's possible response?
c) What was Eliakim warned against (vv. 23-25 GNB)?

NOTES

Amidst the tragic picture of judgment on the nations, Isaiah sets hope for others. He has seen Africans coming to Israel's God with thanksgiving for deliverance. God's mercy will also extend to Egypt and even to what remains of Assyria.

God does control history. If we truly believe that, we will look on current wars and catastrophes in a very different light. Human nature being human, it is easy to agree with the sceptic who says, 'How can a God of love allow these terrible things to happen?'

The Christian's mainstay in this world of turmoil is voiced in the hymn:

Jesus, Jesus how I trust Him;
How I've proved Him o'er and o'er;
Jesus, Jesus, precious Jesus;
Oh for grace to trust Him more.

From God's dealings with Israel we can see that it is futile to trust in men. Ahaz and his people after him had done that and came unstuck. These nations, Babylon, Edom, Arabia and Tyre, both great and small, begin to fall, one by one, as God works out His plan. God is in control.

Ironically, while Isaiah keeps proclaiming the power and purpose of God, most of the people of Jerusalem seem not to take it all in and now Assyria attacks. But the people just want to eat, drink and be merry, closing their eyes (and minds) to reality and hoping vainly that the worst wouldn't happen.

Shebna was typical. He was evidently rich, possibly helping himself to the treasury! He made a great show of his wealth and was sternly warned that his days of power were numbered. Eliakim was to replace Shebna. He was evidently a good man but was eventually brought down because his family used his influence to their own ends.

People do ignore the signs of the times. They ignore and often scorn the voice of God's messengers as they seek to warn them of God's judgment ahead (Acts 17:31). How concerned are we, as God's children, to be involved in God's priority of warning others of their peril (Heb. 10:29-31) and praying earnestly for the fulfilment of His purposes in this world (see the example of Samuel in 1 Sam. 12:23)?

STUDY 8
FROM PRIDE TO PRAISE AND PEACE

QUESTIONS

DAY 1 *Isaiah 23:1-14.*
Who planned Tyre's downfall and why (v. 9)?

DAY 2 *Isaiah 23:15-18.*
What would eventually happen to Tyre (v. 17)?

DAY 3 *Isaiah 24:1-16a.*
a) What is the attitude of the remnant who survive judgment (vv. 14, 15)?
b) Where would God be glorified?

DAY 4 *Isaiah 24:16b-23.*
a) Why does the prophet seem to be unable to join the song of praise (v. 21, 22)?
b) What is the climax in this chapter of judgment (v. 23)? (See also Matt. 25:31, 32; Ps. 86:9, 10.)

DAY 5 *Isaiah 25:1-12.*
a) What message is there for those who oppress God's people (vv. 11, 12)?
b) What is the message for the oppressed (v. 8)? (See also Rev. 21:3, 4.)

DAY 6 *Isaiah 26:1-6.*
a) What great promise is given in verse 3?
b) What is shown to be the guarantee of this promise (v. 4)?

DAY 7 *Isaiah 26:7-11.*
In his prayer Isaiah puts forward a good reason (v. 9) for God's intervention in judgment. Discuss this.

Memory Verse: Isaiah 26:3.

NOTES

Tyre

As Babylon opened the section of God's judgment of the nations (Isa. 13), now Tyre brings it to a close. Like Babylon (see especially Rev. 18:10-24), Tyre is used in a representative way. Babylon's greatness was in its very glory and culture. Tyre's was in its wealth and vast maritime contacts. Together they represented what must have seemed all that was important to many in Isaiah's world.

Isaiah's message here is quite clear: all the nations of the world are completely insignificant and unreliable. Our only hope is to trust in God.

Historians can cite five times when Tyre was under attack from the time of Isaiah to Alexander's well known conquest in 332 BC. Probably Nebuchadnezzar's onslaught is in view here, as also prophesied in Ezekiel 26.

Tyre's pride led to her fall, from which she has never recovered. Even so, a measure of restoration is promised and chapter 23 ends with the picture of Tyre's wealth being used ultimately for God's people.

Judgment

From the more immediate judgment of the nations of Isaiah's day, the prophet moves to the final triumph of God for His people. A contrast is drawn between the City of Man and the City of God. In chapter 24 the major focus is on the city of this world and its overthrow, while chapter 25 gives the prophet's response to its overthrow.

Chapter 24, then, stands as a transition between chapters 13-23 and 25-27. Here all the nations are treated as one, and God is shown as the One who determines the fate of nations in accordance with how they appear in the light of His law (vv. 1, 2, 3, 5, 14, 21).

Peace

Chapter 25 is a hymn of praise in anticipation of the Lord's great victory. The world here acknowledges the power of Israel's God, a fact that will one day be heralded by our Lord's return in glory (Phil. 2:10). This acknowledgement is followed by a festive occasion signifying joy for God's people everywhere as suffering and death are finally eliminated (2 Tim. 1:10; 1 Cor. 15:54; Rev. 21:4).

The end of Moab is probably used as typical of the fate of all God's enemies. Malachi 1:1-5 gives a clear picture of the downfall of Edom.

Isaiah 26 continues the song of praise with, perhaps, more emphasis on the meaning of God's victory for God's people. Here we have the great promise of peace. When we look on the restlessness and suffering in our generation, many doubt whether things will get better. But the perfect peace of God is offered to all who will make their personal peace with God, through Christ. When we put our trust in Him He gives 'the peace that transcends all understanding' (Phil. 4:7), a peace which no-one and no circumstance can take from us as we walk in fellowship with Him.

> Peace, perfect peace
> The future all unknown?
> Jesus we know
> And He is on the throne.

(Edward Henry Bickerstith)

STUDY 9
GOD KNOWS US AND PLANS FOR OUR GOOD

QUESTIONS

DAY 1 *Isaiah 26:12-21.*
a) Compare the end of the foreign oppressor (v. 14) with that of the Lord's people (vv. 12, 19).
b) Read the words of Christ in John 5:25-29. What light do they give on verse 19?

DAY 2 *Isaiah 27:1-6.*
a) Compare and contrast this passage with Isaiah 5:1-7.
b) What do we learn about God's care for His people?

DAY 3 *Isaiah 27:7-13.*
a) What sign does God require of Israel before He can restore her to favour (v. 9)?
b) What two pictures are given to represent Israel's return to their land (vv. 12, 13)?
c) In the light of 1 Corinthians 11:31-32 and Hebrews 12:5-11, discuss how God deals with His people today.

DAY 4 *Isaiah 28:1-13.*
a) What consequences are noted from over indulgence in wine (vv. 7, 8)?
b) Why did these people complain about straightforward preaching (v. 9)?
c) How would God respond to their complaints (v. 11)?

DAY 5 *Isaiah 28:14-22; Romans 9:33; 1 Peter 2:4-6.*
a) How do the apostles interpret the promise of verse 16 more fully?
b) What would happen to Judah's boasted plans (v. 17)?
c) What would the proverbial saying of verse 20 mean for them?

DAY 6 *Isaiah 28:23-29.*
a) This parable teaches a lesson about God's dealings with His people. What is it?
b) What does God want to see in our lives (John 15:1-4; Heb. 12:11)?

QUESTIONS (contd.)

DAY 7 *Isaiah 29:1-12.*
a) When God's people refuse to change, what will God do (v. 2)?
b) When God promises protection as well as judgment how do the people react (vv. 9-12)?

Memory Verse: Isaiah 28:16.

NOTES

Back again to Isaiah's own time! He was God's true prophet. There were others who took that name and only brought Him shame. In fact, both prophets and priests are condemned here for drunkenness and refusal to listen to God. Isaiah warned them: 'You may disregard the word God is speaking, but His judgments on you will teach you why His ways are best.' He denounces their covenant with death and declares that God is laying a firm foundation for faith – the cornerstone which will endure for ever.

In a beautiful picture of a farmer dealing with his seeds and crops, Isaiah depicts God dealing with his people just as carefully and purposefully. He shows how Jerusalem must be humbled if God's people are to learn to turn back to Him.

Despite all these warnings, the people still think they know better than God. Egypt would be their saviour – why not make an alliance with her? It is obvious that they are not hearing God's word through Isaiah or they wouldn't resort to such futile planning. All they want to hear from the prophets is good news – not truth.

In our hearts we may condemn this past generation for their blindness and stubbornness. But aren't we all prone, especially when we get in a tight corner, to rely on our own wits to get us out of the crisis? We are so earth bound, always wanting to SEE the way through, that we forget that the key is FAITH AND TRUST in our all-wise Heavenly Father. The Bible says our thoughts and planning are to be orientated 'in the heavenly realms' (Eph. 2:6) and not by the wisdom of men. Look at 2 Corinthians 5:7: 'We live by faith, not by sight'. Hebrews 11:1 declares: 'Now faith is being sure of what we hope for and CERTAIN of what we DO NOT SEE'. (Only a close, trusting, obedient walk with God brings us into that secure position of faith which is the purchased possession of every believer.)

God does know best. As parents we often have to discipline our children in order to train them to walk wisely. God treats us in just this same way – always in love and always in His all-knowing wisdom – each of us according to our needs. The worst thing we can do is rebel against His loving plans for us.

I am not skilled to understand,
what God has willed, what God has planned.
I only know, at His right hand
Stands One who is my Saviour.
                    Dora Greenwell.

STUDY 10
GOD LONGS TO BLESS US

QUESTIONS

DAY 1 *Isaiah 29:13-16; Matthew 15:7-9.*
a) What judgment will come in response to the nation's hypocrisy (v. 14)?
b) Just what are the plotters of verse 15 denying by their actions (Ps. 139:1-12)?

DAY 2 *Isaiah 29:17-24.*
a) Discuss the effect these transformations would have on Israel (vv. 22, 23).
b) Compare the great reversals promised in verse 8 with what happened during the ministry of Jesus (Matt. 11:4-6). What did they prove?

DAY 3 *Isaiah 30:1-14.*
a) What were the two foolish ingredients in Judah's proposed alliance with Egypt (vv. 1, 2)?
b) What did Judah do instead of listening to God's prophets (v. 10; Matt. 23:37)?
c) What picture is given to show the results of this folly?

DAY 4 *Isaiah 30:15-26.*
a) Find at least three wonderful promises in these verses.
b) What was the purpose behind the hardships of verse 20?

DAY 5 *Isaiah 30:27-33.*
a) Which nation in particular will feel the force of God's wrath here (v. 31)?
b) Compare verse 28 with Isaiah 8:7, 8. What confidence does this give concerning God's judgments and power?

DAY 6 *Isaiah 31.*
a) Why is God's help to be preferred to other kinds of help?
b) Compare verses 4 and 5 with Deuteronomy 32:9-11 and Psalm 91:4. What is the contrasting picture of the Lord's care given in these verses? Note that though Isaiah 31:4 can be used in different ways, it still illustrates God's overall care and protection for His people.

QUESTIONS (contd.)

DAY 7 *Isaiah 32:1-8.*
a) What are the practical results given here of having a righteous ruler?
b) What do the foolish do (vv. 6, 7)?

Memory Verse: Isaiah 30:21.

NOTES

How do you feel when you have loved, advised and sought to guide a child faced with a dilemma, and then see him reject your help and take his own course? Don't you agonise with him when he decides wrongly and brings multiplied problems on his head?

Isaiah must have been so frustrated as he saw Israel's leaders counter his advice and enter into wrong alliances (Isa. 28). He cried out that their only non-fail foundation for security was the precious cornerstone (28:16). The New Testament tells us that this Cornerstone is Jesus (Matt. 21:42; Eph. 2:20; I Pet. 2:7) and we are told to build on Him (I Cor. 3:10-11).

Maybe you remember times when you have disbelieved God's Word, rejected the wise counsel of a Christian friend and so reaped a wrong harvest! Isaiah pleaded (30:15): 'In repentance and rest is your salvation, in quietness and trust is your strength, but YOU WOULD HAVE NONE OF IT'.

What did God offer (30:19-25)?

no more tears,
great grace,
answered prayer,
divine teaching,
correct guidance,
no more idolatry,
good harvests and rich pastures,
all enemies defeated,
singing and rejoicing!

The culmination, of course (v. 26) is His coming, with healing in His wings (Mal. 4:2).

Poor, wayward Israel. Poor wayward any of us who fail to see God's great love in all His dealings with us. Israel looked for a perfect human king, a utopia on earth. God was waiting for them to enthrone Him, the King of Kings in their hearts and to forsake their sinful, rebellious ways. One day, all that God has promised will come to pass. Meanwhile, our patient and gracious God yearns and pleads, 'Come back to Me'. What amazing love!

STUDY 11
THE LORD IS KING

DAY 1 *Isaiah 32:9-20.*
a) What must come before the outpouring of God's Spirit (v. 11)?
b) What are the main results seen here of such an intervention (vv. 15-20)?

DAY 2 *Isaiah 33:1-16* (see also 2 Kings 18:14-17 for probable context).
a) What does verse 6 say about treasure?
b) Apart from Israel's enemies, who else is warned here (v. 14)?

DAY 3 *Isaiah 33:17-24.*
a) While Hezekiah the actual king is doubtless referred to in verse 17, who is really being described (vv. 17-22)?
b) When the Lord reigns absolutely, what will be absent from the city?

DAY 4 *Isaiah 34:1-4.*
a) In this scene of final judgment who are called to hear?
b) What are the nations compared with here (v. 4)?

DAY 5 *Isaiah 34:5-17.*
a) Which nation here is given as an example of God's wrath?
b) What reason does verse 8 give for this judgment?
c) Why could Edom's destruction be viewed as certain (v. 16)?

DAY 6 *Isaiah 35.*
a) What great changes are promised for the desert, the faint-hearted and the disabled?
b) How can verses 8, 9 help those in difficult situations?
c) Share any experience you have had of a need met.

DAY 7 *Isaiah 36:1-12.*
a) Make a list of the tactics used by Sennacherib's representatives here.
b) Compare them with Satan's tactics today (1 Pet. 5:8, 9; Eph. 6:10-19).

Memory Verse: Isaiah 35:10.

NOTES

It is interesting to note the sequences of emphasis the prophet has maintained throughout the book and again demonstrated in chapter 33. First there is confidence, then prayer and trust expressed, followed by the chaos of invasion, then the Lord's intervention. The ungodly react and the prophet's admonition to return to the Lord is repeated.

If the forward look at the end of chapter 33 relates to the partial glory of Hezekiah's reign, it also looks forward to the coming of the King of Kings: 'the Lord is our king; it is he who will save us' (v. 22).

One day we know that every knee will bow to Him. What a priceless privilege we have of acknowledging Him as our King, Lord and Saviour today. With that privilege comes the challenge to share the Good News because there are still millions who have never heard. 'The Lord is angry with all the nations ... He has condemned them to destruction' (Isa. 34:2 GNB.)

Edom, descended from Esau (Gen. 36; I Chron. I:35), is quite often taken as representative of those who knowingly defy God and His servants but verse 2 is universally applied here.

Home

Don't we all love to return to our homes? In Isaiah 35 Israel is returning home to Jerusalem singing joyously. They have yet to fully comprehend that their true home is in heaven (Heb. I3:14) where God reigns supreme. It is good for us to remember that this world is not our home – we are just passing through and are citizens of the Heavenly Jerusalem.

History

Hezekiah at first, albeit unwillingly, followed his father's footsteps in paying tribute to Assyria (2 Kings I8:13-I5). Now, supported by Isaiah, he stands firm and we have in these chapters the reversal of chapters 7, 8.

'The Assyrian came down like a wolf on the fold, And his cohorts were gleaming in purple and gold' (Lord Byron).

Yet God had promised to save Jerusalem from Assyria, so Isaiah and Hezekiah put their faith in God's Word.

STUDY 12
DON'T BE AFRAID

QUESTIONS

DAY 1 *Isaiah 36:13-22.*
a) What false promise did Sennacherib's commander make (v. 16)?
b) How did he insult the Lord God of Israel (v. 18)?

DAY 2 *Isaiah 37:1-7.*
a) How did Hezekiah react to the Assyrian threats?
b) How did Isaiah react?

DAY 3 *Isaiah 37:8-20.*
a) How did Hezekiah react to further threats?
b) Why did he believe his God to be stronger than all other supposed gods (vv. 19, 20)?

DAY 4 *Isaiah 37:21-38.*
a) Who is really being attacked when God's people are taunted (vv. 28, 29)?
b) How did God's word against Sennacherib (v. 34) work out (vv. 36-38)?

DAY 5 *Isaiah 38:1-8.*
a) What reason(s) did God give for extending Hezekiah's life?
b) What miracle would signify that God would keep his promise?

DAY 6 *Isaiah 38:9-22.*
What was Hezekiah's response to God's healing (vv. 15, 20)?

DAY 7 *Isaiah 39.*
a) What do you see as Hezekiah's mistake here (v. 2)?
b) Was his reply to Isaiah's prophecy wrong (v. 8)?

Memory verse: Isaiah 37:20.

NOTES

Have you ever tried to carry water in a bucket riddled with holes? You get very wet, leave a messy trail and arrive at your destination with an empty bucket!

This is just what Judah's futile attempts to liaise with Assyria and Egypt came to. Hezekiah tried to 'buy off' Sennacherib, even stripping gold from the temple to pay his demands. Despite the gift, the Assyrians still advanced on Jerusalem. So Hezekiah sends his envoys to bargain again. All they get is ridicule, the maligning of their king, the tearing down of Isaiah's character and a tirade against Israel's God. The picture just could not be blacker! The envoys return grief-stricken, with their clothes torn and indignant over the threat to Jerusalem and the enemy's demand that they surrender. Hezekiah mourns in the same way at their news, yet he turns to His God, demonstrating himself to be God's man in this distress.

Isaiah had already sought the Lord and declared His Word: 'Don't be afraid. I will rout Sennacherib – he will return to his own country and will be killed' (37:5-7).

That prophecy came to pass (37:36-38)! Hezekiah and his forces did not have to deal one blow to the enemy. The Lord supernaturally wiped out 185,000 men in one night. We don't know how – maybe by a plague – but it was God's doing. God's angel of death destroyed the whole army.

> Like the leaves of the forest when summer is green,
> That host with their banners at sunset were seen:
> Like the leaves of the forest when Autumn has blown
> the host on the morrow lay withered and strown.
>
> (Lord Byron)

In the face of God's predictions through Isaiah the historic account in 2 Kings 19 makes interesting reading. Look at it before starting the study on Isaiah 40-66.

Two messages from the Lord stand out clearly as we finish this section. Hezekiah had to prove them in his own personal health crisis (2 Kings 20:1-11) and so, by the grace of God, lived another fifteen years!

'Stand still and see the salvation of God. Do not be afraid.' These words strengthen me to go on praising God in my daily life no matter what problems I have to face. Do they encourage you?

ANSWER GUIDE

The following pages contain an Answer Guide. It is recommended that answers to the questions be attempted before turning to this guide. It is only a guide and the answers given should not be treated as exhaustive.

GUIDE TO INTRODUCTORY STUDY

The name Isaiah means 'Salvation of Jehovah' and is almost identical in meaning with Hoshna – 'Jehovah is Salvation'. Down the years 'Isaiah' became 'Joshua' then 'Jeshua' and finally 'Jesus' meaning the 'Lord is Salvation' (Matt. 1:21).

Answers to the quiz reveal that Isaiah lived in the Southern Kingdom of Judah. His wife was a prophetess and bore him Shear-Jashub (meaning 'a remnant will return') and Maher-Shalal-Hash-Baz (meaning 'the spoil speeds, the prey hastens'). Called to be God's messenger to a defaulting nation, his witness spanned the reigns of four kings and he fearlessly denounced his people for, in both word and deed, they denied the sovereignty of God. Surely God's judgment must fall on such a disobedient and rebellious nation. Yet he preached a message of hope – the coming of Immanuel, the child of a virgin who would one day rule with authority and power and be acknowledged as the Wonderful Counsellor, Mighty God, Everlasting Father and Prince of Peace.

'Rabbinic tradition has it that Isaiah's father, Amoz (not Amos the prophet) was a brother of King Amaziah. This would make Isaiah first cousin to King Uzziah, and grandson of King Joash, and thus of royal blood ... He wrote other books ... (2 Chron. 26:22 and 32:32). He is quoted in the New Testament more than any other prophet ... A tradition in the Talmud (Jewish writings of the early Christian centuries) which was accepted as authentic by early Church Fathers, states that Isaiah resisted Manasseh's idolatrous decrees, and was fastened between two planks, and "sawn asunder" thus suffering a most horrible death. This is thought to be referred to in Hebrews 11:37' (extract from Halley's Bible Handbook, p. 285).

An interesting fact, which confirms the integrity of the Bible, was the discovery in 1947 of a scroll by an Arab Bedouin as he searched for a lost sheep. Near the Dead Sea he came upon a partially collapsed cave. It had obviously been used to preserve, in sealed earthenware jars, part of a Jewish library, probably at the time of the Roman conquest of Judea. One of these scrolls was the Book of Isaiah, written 2,000 years ago – 1,000 years older than any known manuscript of the Hebrew Old Testament! The oldest known books then were made about 900 AD.

The 2,000 year old manuscript is essentially the same as the Book of Isaiah in our Bible today.

As you lead this group in their study of Isaiah, share some of the above facts with them and do use maps, etc. to help them understand the geography of the time of Isaiah. Encourage memory work as you go through Isaiah – it is full of marvellous promises, etc.

Warn the group members that there will be longer daily/weekly portions to read in preparation of the studies. Isaiah is a long book. It would be impossible to cover it adequately in a ten week course. To cut down on reading almost demands that we divide it into 3 x 10 week courses. We have chosen to do it in 2 x 12 week courses, hence some lessons require that we tackle more than average daily portions. However, to understand these studies it is vital that all the assigned scriptures be read. By all means use various modern translations along with your regular translation to help in understanding the story.

GUIDE TO STUDY 1

DAY 1   a) Dumb animals know their master, but the people of God, reared and instructed by Him, do not know Him.
b) Like Sodom and Gomorrah, Judah would be judged but would not be completely destroyed.

DAY 2   a) The rulers and people of Judah.
b) Disgust and weariness because of their meaningless sacrifices and continual sinning.

DAY 3   a) Injustice and lack of concern for the helpless.
b) Verse 18. God still offers complete cleansing and forgiveness.

DAY 4   a) An unfaithful woman; impure silver; watered-down wine.
b) Bribery and idolatry
c) Cleansing and forgiveness; restoration of righteousness.

DAY 5   a) No. The early Church was to set out from Jerusalem to spread the gospel.
b) The picture of the Heavenly New Jerusalem with its welcome corresponds well to one fulfilment of Isaiah's vision.

DAY 6   a) The challenge to walk in the light of the Lord. God's Word is light; obedience to it enables this challenge to be fulfilled.
b) Idolatry, magic, pride and arrogance. God would humble them.

DAY 7   The nation of Israel: the proud and mighty and those who trusted in idols.

Leaders: Have the group repeat together several times Isaiah 1:18 and encourage them to memorise it – it is a key scripture.

GUIDE TO STUDY 2

DAY 1 a) Immature leadership, unwillingness to lead, oppression of the poor and open sinning.
b) The righteous.
c) The elders and leaders.

DAY 2 a) Their arrogance. They had an extravagant lifestyle no doubt obtained at the expense of the poor.
b) Not being able to marry: shortage of men would make them go to any length to bribe a man to marry them.

DAY 3 a) The Lord.
b) God would protect it and provide shelter for its people.

DAY 4 a) It yielded only poor fruit.
b) An abundance of good fruit (Gal. 5:22, 23).
c) Injustice and oppression.

DAY 5 a) Greed and over indulgence in wine.
b) Poverty, drought, captivity, death.

DAY 6 a) Mockery of God's law and the prophets; drinking; pride; reversal of values; injustice; accepting bribes.
b) Rejection of God's commands.
c) Personal. Encourage discussion on any points offered.

DAY 7 a) War
b) Assyria.

Read Isaiah 4:5-6 together and encourage the group to memorise it.

GUIDE TO STUDY 3

DAY 1
a) His vision of God's holiness and glory.
b) With cleansing and an assurance of forgiveness.
c) What Isaiah experienced: cleansing and forgiveness.

DAY 2
a) He heard God's call and responded to it. (Note that there was vision (v. 1); conviction (v. 5); cleansing (v. 7); challenge and commission (v. 8). This is still God's way of dealing with us but 'vision' is usually revelation through God's Word.)
b) No. The unbelief of the Jews to the message of the gospel in his day.

DAY 3
a) As smouldering pieces of firewood.
b) Though apparently causing terror he was not to be regarded as very important.
c) Faith and the abili to stay alert and calm when being provoked.

DAY 4
a) Christ's virgin birth is foretold and His name declared.
b) Immanuel means God with us, that is, God come in the flesh.

DAY 5
a) As an invasion of flies and bees and the use of a razor.
b) The Lord. The Lord controls those who oppress His people.
c) King Ahaz had asked Assyria to help Judah defeat her enemies!

DAY 6
a) Just as Assyria invaded Aram (Syria) and Israel, as predicted.
b) As a river in flood.
c) Judah would not be totally submerged.

DAY 7
a) 'God is with us'. Immanuel.
b) Consult mediums and dabble in the occult (clearly forbidden in the Bible).
c) The Word of God to instruct and guide.

GUIDE TO STUDY 4

DAY 1   a) Distress, darkness, fear of death, oppression, bloodshed, etc.
b) Wonderful (beyond imagination), Counsellor (ready to guide), Mighty God (all powerful), Everlasting Father (eternally caring/loving the world).

DAY 2   a) Defiance, arrogance, deception on the part of leaders.
b) God's anger was still present and His hand still upraised (vv. 12, 17, 21).

DAY 3   a) That of being a tool to punish Israel.
b) She would attempt to destroy Judah – not just God's tool to punish.
c) God disciplines us for our good – to make us better and stronger Christians.

DAY 4   a) By reminding her how lowly her position was and how absurd her claims were.
b) Very little!

DAY 5   a) Probably the crossing of the Red Sea (Exod. 7:19). Also Gideon's defeat of the Midianites at the rock of Oreb (Judg. 7:24, 25).
b) The Lord. He will be like a woodcutter chopping down trees.

DAY 6   a) Under the control of the Spirit of God, wise, understanding, a righteous judge who destroys the wicked and brings about universal peace and contentment.
b) The Spirit of God will uphold Him. He will punish the wicked.
c) Peace and harmony between the animals and also between humans and animals. Total lack of fear.

DAY 7   a) People will be united as they rally to the Messiah, the Root of Jesse (Rom. 15:12).
b) To the return of Israel from Egypt under Moses.

GUIDE TO STUDY 5

DAY 1   a) With trust in God, deliverance from fear, happiness and a desire to share with others what God has done.
b) Yes. If we know Him, these should also characterise our lives.

DAY 2   a) God is calling His armies (seen and unseen) to defeat Babylon.
b) We should never lose sight of the fact that Christian warfare is against the forces of evil – not people.

DAY 3   The Day of the Lord/the Day of Judgment.

DAY 4   a) Pride and arrogance.
b) It will be completely overthrown and left desolate.

DAY 5   a) One day they will return to their own land and they will be acknowledged as God's special people.
b) The Lord.

DAY 6   a) Peace would come to the nations through the downfall of the oppressor who had presumed to be like God.
b) The serpent in Eden also presumed to be equal with God, and this is Satan's claim throughout the Bible (vv. 12-14 show this clearly). See also Ezekiel 28:1, 2, 14-16 regarding the King of Tyre.

DAY 7   a) God will crush them and deliver Israel out of their hands.
b) God is in total control and will bring His purposes to pass, not only nationally, but personally (2 Tim. 4:18).

GUIDE TO STUDY 6

Leaders: Make sure you have a map and locate for your group the various countries/
tribes mentioned in this study.

DAY 1   a) Isaiah's heart aches in sympathy for Moab and her fate.
         b) Jesus did and Paul did and so should we.

DAY 2   a) They will also come under the righteous rule of the coming
         King.
         b) Their pride and arrogance stand in the way.

DAY 3   a) Their religion.
         b) Personal

DAY 4   a) The country, represented by its capital Damascus, would be in
         ruins.
         b) A wasting disease; corn being cut down; olives being harvested.

DAY 5   a) The people will return to honour God and will turn away from
         idols.
         b) The events of the settlement under Joshua and the Judges when
         the Canaanite cities were captured.
         c) They have forgotten the Lord their God.

DAY 6   a) A raging sea.
         b) Chaff driven by the wind.

DAY 7   The people coming to worship the Lord.
         The Ethiopian eunuch becomes a believer.

GUIDE TO STUDY 7

DAY 1 a) Through civil war, confusion, drought, oppression, famine, poverty and a sense of helplessness.
b) Their wise men. (I Cor. I:18-25 quotes from Isa. 19. This passage further illustrates the difference between God's wisdom and 'wise' men especially in relation to the cross.)

DAY 2 a) Probably because of what God does for His own people.
b) Their turning to God and His blessing on them.

DAY 3 a) His actions demonstrated the failure of a revolt against Assyria and the fate that awaited Egypt and Cush.
b) They would realise that these nations could not help them.
c) On God, their Rock and Saviour.

DAY 4 a) He is staggered and horrified.
b) Babylon has fallen.

DAY 5 a) The need for patient endurance.
b) No definite time for God's judgment is known to us (Mark 13:32 -37).

DAY 6 a) In a hopeless condition they were relying on human resources and endeavour; instead of repenting they were making merry and trying to drown their sorrows in drink.
b) He would not forgive them.

DAY 7 a) His costly tomb showed his arrogance toward God at a time when a humble attitude was essential.
b) It is likely that he did repent and was reinstated to a lower position.
c) Against his family taking advantage of his high office.

GUIDE TO STUDY 8

DAY 1   The Lord Almighty. Because of her pride rooted in materialism.

DAY 2   She apparently returned to her former life of barter and trade, but her income was used to help God's people.
(Note that the figure of prostitution was often used simply as a derogatory reference to trade and moneymaking.)

DAY 3   a) They praise the God of Israel,
b) Throughout all the earth!

DAY 4   a) Isaiah is deeply affected by God's judgments and feels himself still to be suffering with the afflicted.
b) God, the Almighty reigning.

DAY 5   a) In God's time they will cease to exist.
b) God will one day take away all sorrow and death.

DAY 6   a) Trust in God brings perfect peace.
b) The Lord is an Eternal Rock, our strong Protector.

DAY 7   People must learn what justice is. If kindness alone were shown to the wicked, how could they learn what is right?

GUIDE TO STUDY 9

DAY 1 a) They die and are forgotten, whereas God's people will one day be resurrected to eternal life (John 6:40).
b) The resurrection will be in God's time and will divide the righteous from the unrighteous (I Thess. 5:1-11).

DAY 2 a) The vineyard in chapter 5 was to be destroyed because it bore sour grapes. Here the vineyard is fruitful.
b) God's discipline is for the good of His people. He never will completely forsake them.

DAY 3 a) They must abandon worship of idols – and show this by destroying them.
b) The careful bringing in of a harvest after threshing, and the sounding of a trumpet to call His people to worship in Jerusalem.
c) As in DAY 2b (above): God's discipline is for our good.

DAY 4 a) Helplessness, confusion, vomiting, etc.
b) It was too easy and simple for them; God was treating them like children.
c) God would send foreigners to teach them a much harder lesson if they would not listen to His words.

DAY 5 a) Jesus Christ is this solid cornerstone and foundation of faith.
b) Everything they were relying on would be swept away.
c) Whatever protection they were expecting would not be enough.

DAY 6 a) God is wise in His dealings; He is working towards a specific goal in mind.
b) Much fruit (Gal. 5:22, 23).

DAY 7 a) He will bring some form of trial or disaster as a warning.
b) They just cannot understand what God is saying to them, so disregard it.

GUIDE TO STUDY 10

DAY 1
a) A series of signs/wonders that they could not possibly have foreseen.
b) That God sees and knows everything; they are pretending to know better than their Creator.

DAY 2
a) They would no longer be ashamed or in disgrace; they would acknowledge the God of Israel and honour Him.
b) The miracles of Jesus were proof that He was indeed the promised Messiah.

DAY 3
a) Not asking God for guidance and looking for help from a nation that was known to be unreliable.
b) Looked for other prophets who would tell them what they wanted to hear; they persecuted them. (Compare 2 Tim. 4:3,4)
c) A wall with a hole in it – a picture of imminent disaster. A broken pot – they too would be shattered and useless.

DAY 4
a) Salvation and strength through repentance and trust (v. 15); compassion to be shown (v. 18); prayers answered (v. 19).
b) God was longing to restore and bless the people.

DAY 5
a) Assyria
b) God is totally in control of everything and His justice will prevail.

DAY 6
a) God is all-wise and powerful; Egypt's help and reliance on horses are nothing compared to God's intervention.
b) He is like a lion in strength and yet protects as tenderly as a bird watches over its young.

DAY 7
a) Justice, protection, provision, consideration for all are in operation.
b) Persecute and treat unfairly the most needy and helpless.

GUIDE TO STUDY 11

DAY 1   a) A genuine sorrow for sin and repentance indicated by a willingness to leave behind the luxuries of the past.
b) The land would become fertile and prosperous; righteousness, justice, peace and security would reign.

DAY 2   a) The key to God's treasure is the fear of the Lord.
b) The sinners among God's people.

DAY 3   a) The Lord.
b) Foreign officials who dominate, take their money and cause terror; sickness and guilt for past sins.

DAY 4   a) All the nations of the earth.
b) The stars of heaven, withered vine leaves and shrivelled figs.

DAY 5   a) Edom
b) Edom was an implacable enemy of Israel and God would intervene on behalf of His people.
c) It had been decreed by God; it was in His 'scroll' (probably as in Ps. 40:7; Dan. 7:10; Mal. 3:16; and Rev. 20:12).

DAY 6   a) The desert will blossom and flow with water; the fainthearted will be strengthened; the disabled will be healed.
b) They tell of God's special care for His redeemed people.
c) Personal

DAY 7   a) He tried to instil doubt about help from Egypt; doubt about help from God (Hezekiah had only destroyed false altars); doubt about their ability to withstand Assyria. There was the suggestion that Assyria was being helped by God to destroy Judah.
b) General discussion.

GUIDE TO STUDY 12

DAY 1 a) He said they would enjoy peace and prosperity under Assyrian rule.
b) He put God alongside the gods of the other nations and said that He could not save Jerusalem from Assyria.

DAY 2 a) With a mixture of fear and yet a faint glimmer of hope and trust; he tore his clothes but then went into the temple.
b) He told Hezekiah not to be afraid.

DAY 3 a) He spread the Assyrian letter before the Lord and prayed.
b) Other people's gods were only human in origin and made of wood and stone. His God was the only true God.

DAY 4 a) The Lord.
b) His army was wiped out by the angel of the Lord and he fled back to Nineveh where his sons assassinated him. He never did enter Jerusalem.

DAY 5 a) God had heard his prayer and seen his tears and would deliver him and the city from the King of Assyria.
b) The sun's shadow would go back ten steps (2 Kings 20:8-11).

DAY 6 He vowed to walk humbly for the rest of his life and to continually praise and worship the Lord.

DAY 7 a) He displayed pride in his possessions, and gave the Babylonians a chance to assess his strength if and when they might decide to attack Jerusalem.
b) Yes. He seems only to have thought of his own safety.

THE WORD WORLDWIDE

We first heard of WORD WORLDWIDE over 20 years ago when Marie Dinnen, its founder, shared excitedly about the wonderful way ministry to one needy woman had exploded to touch many lives. It was great to see the Word of God being made central in the lives of thousands of men and women, then to witness the life-changing results of them applying the Word to their circumstances. Over the years the vision for WORD WORLDWIDE has not dimmed in the hearts of those who are involved in this ministry. God is still at work through His Word and in today's self-seeking society, the Word is even more relevant to those who desire true meaning and purpose in life. WORD WORLDWIDE is a ministry of WEC International, an interdenominational missionary society, whose sole purpose is to see Christ known, loved and worshipped by all, particularly those who have yet to hear of His wonderful name. This ministry is a vital part of our work and we warmly recommend the WORD WORLDWIDE 'Geared for Growth' Bible studies to you. We know that as you study His Word you will be enriched in your personal walk with Christ. It is our hope that as you are blessed through these studies, you will find opportunities to help others discover a personal relationship with Jesus. As a mission we would encourage you to work with us to make Christ known to the ends of the earth.

Stewart and Jean Moulds – British Directors, **WEC International**.

A full list of over 50 'Geared for Growth' studies can be obtained from:

ENGLAND   John and Ann Edwards
5 Louvain Terrace, Hetton-le-Hole, Tyne & Wear, DH5 9PP
Tel. 0191 5262803 Email: rhysjohn.edwards@virgin.net

IRELAND   Steffney Preston
33 Harcourts Hill, Portadown, Craigavon, N. Ireland, BT62 3RE
Tel. 028 3833 7844 Email: sa.preston@talk21.com

SCOTLAND Margaret Halliday
10 Douglas Drive, Newton Mearns, Glasgow, G77 6HR
Tel. 0141 639 8695 Email: m.halliday@ntlworld.com

WALES   William and Eirian Edwards
Penlan Uchaf, Carmarthen Road, Kidwelly, Carms., SA17 5AF
Tel. 01554 890423 Email: Penlan.uchaf@farming.co.uk

UK CO-ORDINATOR
Anne Jenkins
2 Windermere Road, Carnforth, Lancs., LA5 9AR
Tel. 01524 734797 Email: anne@jenkins.abelgratis.com

UK Website: www.wordworldwide.org.uk

Christian Focus Publications

publishes books for all ages

Our mission statement –

STAYING FAITHFUL

In dependence upon God we seek to help make His infallible word, the Bible, relevant. Our aim is to ensure that the Lord Jesus Christ is presented as the only hope to obtain forgiveness of sin, live a useful life and look forward to heaven with Him.

REACHING OUT

Christ's last command requires us to reach out to our world with His gospel. We seek to help fulfill that by publishing books that point people towards Jesus and help them to develop a Christ-like maturity. We aim to equip all levels of readers for life, work, ministry and mission.

Books in our adult range are published in three imprints.

Christian Focus contains popular works including biographies, commentaries, basic doctrine, and Christian living. Our children's books are also published in this imprint.

Mentor focuses on books written at a level suitable for Bible College and seminary students, pastors, and other serious readers; the imprint includes commentaries, doctrinal studies, examination of current issues, and church history.

Christian Heritage contains classic writings from the past.

For details of our titles visit us on our website
www.christianfocus.com

ISBN 0 908067 55 0

Copyright © WEC International

Published in 2002 by
Christian Focus Publications, Geanies House,
Fearn, Ross-shire, IV20 ITW, Scotland
and
WEC International, Bulstrode, Oxford Road,
Gerrards Cross, Bucks , SL9 8SZ

Cover design by Alister MacInnes

Printed and bound by J.W Arrowsmith, Bristol

Unless otherwise stated, quotations from the Bible are from the New International Version, © 1973, 1978, 1984 by International Bible Society, published in Great Britain by Hodder and Stoughton Ltd.